THIS IS ETERNAL LIFE

RIGHT HERE, RIGHT NOW

NATHANIEL DELISLE

RCCB PRESS

Copyright © Nathaniel Delisle 2025

All rights reserved. No part of this book may be reproduced in any form or by any electronic or mechanical means, including information storage and retrieval systems, without permission in writing from the publisher, except by a reviewer who may quote brief passages in a review.

To request permission please email remnantchristianchurchblair@gmail.com

ISBN Paperback: 979-8-218-77326-7

ISBN e-book: 979-8-218-77327-4

First edition: September 2025

Edited by: Robert Holden

Cover art by: Vickie Swisher

Layout design: Angie McCauley

Proofreading: Barbara Wernicke

RCCB Press

Blair, NE 68008

Unless otherwise indicated, Scripture quotations are from The ESV® Bible (The Holy Bible, English Standard Version®), © 2001 by Crossway, a publishing ministry of Good News Publishers. Used by permission. All rights reserved.

Other Scripture quotations are from the following translations:

The Christian Standard Bible. Copyright © 2017 by Holman Bible Publishers. Used by permission. Christian Standard Bible®, and CSB® are federally registered trademarks of Holman Bible Publishers, all rights reserved.

Amplified Bible (AMP), Copyright © 2015 by The Lockman Foundation, La Habra, CA 90631. All rights reserved.

CONTENTS

Introduction	v
1. In the Beginning	1
2. Created Beings	9
3. Why the Tree?	15
4. The Great Fall	23
5. Redemption Early On	29
6. Atonement	37
7. In Steps Jesus	43
8. The Hardworking Holy Spirit	53
9. Where Do We Go from Here?	59

INTRODUCTION

This book is written for those seeking God and those seeking a greater knowledge of who He is. For those who have never met Him, and for those who've spent a lifetime in church. Jesus said, "For God so loved the world, he sent his only Son, that whoever believes in him should not perish but have eternal life" (John 3:16). He then explains what eternal life is: "And this is eternal life, that they know you, the only true God, and Jesus Christ whom you have sent" (John 17:3).

Jesus doesn't want us to be at all confused about this. I believe it's why He was so straightforward about the whole idea. Eternal life doesn't start when we die. It starts right here and right now. It starts with a right knowledge and understanding of who God is, in all of His glory. It starts with a right relationship with Him that can start at this very moment and run the course of your entire life.

One of my greatest fears is hearing Jesus say to me, "I

never knew you" (Matthew 7:23), and I'm convinced that many don't even think about this reality, let alone understand the gravity of the situation. Jesus said, "Many will say to me on that day, 'Lord, Lord …'" (Matthew 7:22). First, "many" holds the idea that it's a big number of people who won't "know" Him on that day. Second, He's speaking to followers, so He isn't speaking about people who aren't familiar with Him. He goes on to say that those who come to Him claim to have done mighty miracles and many mighty acts in His name, and yet He states, "I never knew you."

This leads to my third point. We don't understand the idea of "know" in the scriptural tense. The Greek word *ginosko* refers to an intimate knowledge, to know absolutely, and far more than a knowledge of existence. Although I know of many famous persons, I do not "know" them personally or intimately. I do, though, know my wife intimately and my children personally. How often I've told my daughters, "I know you very well. Almost better than you know yourself." This is the idea of *ginosko* as Jesus used it. It might be better to word it like this: "Many will come to me on that day saying, 'Look at all we did in Your name!' and I will say to them, 'We had no real relationship. I know your name, but we don't really know each other.'"

My daughter asked recently, "How is that possible? If He created me and knows everything about me, then He knows me!" To which I had to respond, "Having knowledge of someone is not the same thing as having an intimate relationship with them."

So, that is the purpose of this book. To give an understanding of this Most High God, and to introduce Him to you, that you may begin this most wonderful journey of relationship with the creator of all. So, join me as we embark on eternal life, to know the One True God and Jesus Christ, whom He sent.

CHAPTER 1
IN THE BEGINNING

"In the beginning was the Word, and the Word was with God, and the Word was God. He was in the beginning with God. All things were made through him, and without him was not any thing made that was made. In him was life, and the life was the light of men. The light shines in the darkness, and the darkness has not overcome it" (John 1:1–5).

Jesus was there in the beginning. He was there before the beginning. This may be a truth we know, but is it one we believe with all our hearts? Jesus is not just a part of the divine Godhead; He is God in all the ways that make God who He says He is. Jesus was both fully God and fully man. In this chapter, we are going to focus primarily on Jesus being fully God in the beginning. We want to fully see and understand that He is exactly who He says He is.

The Apostle Paul wrote, "For from him and through him and to him are all things. To him be glory forever. Amen" (Romans 11:36), and elsewhere he states that Jesus "though he was in the form of God, did not count equality with God a thing to be grasped" (Philippians 2:6).

These two verses together tell us something important. Jesus is made up of the exact same stuff as His Father. Jesus said, "I and the Father are one" (John 10:30). So He is not only made of the exact same divine stuff but was there in the beginning, and all things that exist do so because of Him, for He holds all things together.

Louie Giglio gave a fantastic example of Jesus holding all things together in one of his specials.[1] If you haven't heard of it before, stop what you are doing and go look up an image of laminin. It is a protein molecule. Its job is to hold the body together. I know some will be skeptical and mock, "You just see Jesus everywhere." You might be right, but that doesn't change the fact that the creator God, through the Apostle Paul, states, "from him and through him and to him."

Here, Paul says it again, "He is the image of the invisible God, the firstborn of all creation. For by him all things were created, in heaven and on earth, visible and invisible, whether thrones or dominions or rulers or authorities—all things were created through him and for him. And he is before all things, and in him all things hold together" (Colossians 1:15–17).

Before continuing, we must understand what Paul is saying. Paul is not saying that Christ is a created being. There are many out in the world that make that claim. But Paul is using the same concept seen in the genealogies found in the Old Testament. Paul is explaining that Jesus is first in preeminence. Preeminence is the idea of having a higher rank, higher

---

1. How Great Is Our God by Pastor Louie Giglio

dignity, or higher importance. Look at Genesis 11 for proof of this idea.

I've heard and seen it taught that each name spoken in every genealogy from Adam till Abram was the firstborn in each lineage. But this simply cannot be true. Seth was not the firstborn of Adam. Noah didn't have triplets that we know of. And Abram was not the firstborn of Terah.

But doesn't that contradict the text from Genesis 11:26? Not if taken in light of preeminence. Abram was first in light of the future Messiah, first in light of honor, rank, and dignity. He was the youngest of Terah's sons and yet the one from whom we get the Son of promise. So Jesus cannot be the first created being, for as Paul wrote, "For by him all things were created." Paul is speaking of Jesus as preeminent above creation as creator of all things, seen and unseen.

Let's walk through a couple more verses. "That their hearts may be encouraged, being knit together in love, to reach all the riches of full assurance of understanding and the knowledge of God's mystery, which is Christ, in whom are hidden all the treasures of wisdom and knowledge. For in him the whole fullness of deity dwells bodily" (Colossians 2:2–3, 9). Once again, this shows that Jesus is not only fully God, but is the wisdom and knowledge of that same God that the world had been (and still is) searching for.

"To the King of the ages, immortal, invisible, the only God, be honor and glory forever and ever. Amen" (1 Timothy 1:17). "But in these last days he has spoken to us by his Son, whom he appointed the heir of all things, through whom also he created the world" (Hebrews 1:2).

I hope it isn't getting old yet, letting the Scripture show us who Jesus is as a part of the Trinity. Letting us fully see all the times and ways that God, through the urging of the Holy Spirit, spoke through human authors to explain how Jesus can be seen since the beginning.

The writer of Hebrews goes so far as to use two different Psalms in his first chapter (Psalms 45 and 102) to show who Jesus is and was since the beginning:

> But of the Son he says, "Your throne, O God, is forever and ever, and the scepter of uprightness is the scepter of your kingdom. You have loved righteousness and hated wickedness; therefore God, your God, has anointed you with the oil of gladness beyond your companions." And, "You, Lord, laid the foundation of the earth in the beginning, and the heavens are the work of your hands; they will perish, but you remain; they will all wear out like a garment, like a robe you will roll them up, like a garment they will be changed. But you are the same, and your years will have no end." (Hebrews 1:8–12)

The writer states it again at the end of his letter: "Jesus Christ is the same yesterday and today and forever" (Hebrews 13:8). So we see that Jesus was talked about in the Old Testament. In this case, specifically the Psalms, Jesus has existed since before the beginning and has never changed. He is the same yesterday, today, and forever. What a wonderful God that we serve.

"That which was from the beginning, which we have heard, which we have seen with our eyes, which we looked upon and have touched with our hands, concerning the word of life—the life was made manifest, and we have seen it, and testify to it and proclaim to you the eternal life, which was with the Father and was made manifest to us—that which we have seen and heard we proclaim also to you, so that you too may have fellowship with us; and indeed our fellowship is with the Father and with his Son Jesus Christ" (1 John 1:1–3).

Note how John starts both his gospel and this letter with "the beginning." John wanted people to know that Jesus is, was, and always will be God. This should no longer even be a question. To those who believe Jesus was just a good man or good teacher who taught some really good moral stuff, that is a flat lie and must be done away with. As C.S. Lewis wrote: Jesus was either a liar, a lunatic, or exactly who He claimed to be.[2]

Lastly, let us look at what God says about Himself, "'I am the Alpha and the Omega,' says the Lord God, 'who is and who was and who is to come, the Almighty'" (Revelation 1:8).

But wait. Jesus says this exact same thing: "I am the Alpha and the Omega, the first and the last, the beginning and the end" (Revelation 22:13). If this doesn't solidify within us that Jesus and the Father are one, I'm not sure what else will. That's not all. Look at what Jesus says about Himself. There are seven times in the gospel of John that record Jesus making certain statements about Himself. They all include this Greek phrase: *ego eimi*. It means "I am," yet would be better translated as "I AM."

For those wondering, why all caps? It's a practice for the purpose of showing honor to the divine name of God. The tetragrammaton YHWH was the name God gave Moses before the burning bush, which we will examine shortly.

Jesus says, "I AM the bread of life" (John 6:35), "I AM the

---

2. C.S. Lewis *Mere Christianity*

light of the world" (John 8:12), "I AM the door" (John 10:7, 9), "I AM the good shepherd" (John 10:11, 14), "I AM the resurrection and the life" (John 11:25), "I AM the way, the truth, and the life" (John 14:6), and "I AM the true vine" (John 15:1, 5). But these aren't the only times He used this phrase, "I AM." They are just the main "I AM" statements.

Jesus speaking to the woman at the well says, "I who speak to you am he" (John 4:26). This phrase in Greek, *ego eimi ho lalon soi* would be better translated as: "I AM speaks to you." The words *ego eimi* to the Jews of Jesus' day were never misunderstood. They knew exactly what He meant when He used this particular phrase. "Jesus said to them, 'Truly, truly, I say to you, before Abraham was, I AM.' So they picked up stones to throw at him, but Jesus hid himself and went out of the temple" (John 8:58–59).

The Jews knew exactly what and who Jesus was talking about. He was announcing to the world that "I and the Father are one" (John 10:30); "you will know that I am in my Father" (John 14:20). This is not at all an exhaustive list of Scriptures to back up what we are discussing here. We haven't even scratched the surface of the Gospels, let alone the Old Testament.

When Jesus used the statement *ego eimi*, He was referencing the name given by God to Moses in Exodus chapter three. Moses was in front of that burning bush, and God said, "I AM the God of your father" (Exodus 3:6) and "I AM WHO I AM" (Exodus 3:14). When we examine this phrasing in the Hebrew language, we get a bigger picture of what God was saying. He was telling Moses, "I'm where everything came from. Before everything else began to exist, I was there. I'm before all things. I exist because I exist."

This may sound slightly confusing, to say I exist because I exist. It shouldn't be, though. God was essentially saying, "Don't worry about where I came from. There is none like me." It was this name (I AM), which God gave to Moses, that Jesus proclaimed in the hearing of any who would listen. Jesus claimed not only to be the Son of God, but to be equal to the Father, essentially saying, "I am the true manifestation of God in human form."

We can fully see and understand why the Jews would have wanted to stone Jesus. If He is making that kind of a claim and they didn't believe that it was even possible for God to step down from His divine form into the form of man, of course they would be appalled.

There is much more that can be explored about this idea. Isaiah prophesied a few times about the complexity of the God that we serve. But in ending this chapter, we will only bring up one to think and pray on. Isaiah 48:16 (CSB) reads, "'Approach me and listen to this. From the beginning I have not spoken in secret; from the time anything existed, I was there.' And now the Lord God has sent me and his Spirit."

Here we see the three different persons; the Lord God, the sent one (Messiah), and the Spirit. The one pleading with Israel states, "I was there in the beginning ... the Lord God has sent me." When we read in the Law of Moses, "Hear, O Israel: The Lord our God, the Lord is one" (Deuteronomy 6:4), we can know with absolute certainty that Jesus is a part of that oneness. He was there in the beginning.

CHAPTER 2
CREATED BEINGS

Back to the beginning again. In the beginning, God created all we see. On the sixth day, after He had created all life on the blue ball we call Earth, He created His crowning achievement.

> Then God said, "Let us make man in our image, after our likeness. And let them have dominion over the fish of the sea and over the birds of the heavens and over the livestock and over all the earth and over every creeping thing that creeps on the earth."
> So God created man in his own image,
> in the image of God he created him;
> male and female he created them.
> And God blessed them. And God said to them, "Be fruitful and multiply and fill the earth and subdue it, and have dominion over the fish of the sea and over the birds of the heavens and over every living thing that

moves on the earth." And God said, "Behold, I have given you every plant yielding seed that is on the face of all the earth, and every tree with seed in its fruit. You shall have them for food. And to every beast of the earth and to every bird of the heavens and to everything that creeps on the earth, everything that has the breath of life, I have given every green plant for food." And it was so. (Genesis 1:26–30)

Let us start with this concept of "the image of God." By now, you know and understand the idea that God made everything from nothing. In general, Christendom doesn't seem to struggle with the concept of *ex nihilo* (from nothing). There was nothing. A void, nothingness. Then BOOM!! Lots of something. But we do struggle with this idea of being created in God's image.

When the Bible says we are created in the image of God, it isn't speaking about a physical image. God is spirit, and as such has no bodily form. When God created us in His image, it was mainly in terms of moral, ethical, and intellectual abilities. We can reason, communicate verbally and nonverbally, create, and build.

According to the Amplified Bible study notes on Genesis 1:26, "A more recent view, based on a possible interpretation of Hebrew grammar and the knowledge of the Middle East, interprets the phrase as meaning 'Let us make man *as* our image.' In ancient times an emperor might command statues of himself to be placed in remote parts of his empire. These symbols would declare that these areas were under his power and reign. So God placed humankind as living symbols of Himself on Earth to represent His reign. This interpretation fits well with the command that follows—to reign over all that God has made."

We read in the Psalms:

When I look at your heavens, the work of your fingers,
the moon and the stars, which you have set in place,
what is man that you are mindful of him,
and the son of man that you care for him?
Yet you have made him a little lower than the heavenly
   beings
and crowned him with glory and honor.
You have given him dominion over all the works of
   your hands;
you have put all things under his feet,
all sheep and oxen,
and also the beasts of the field,
the birds of the heavens, and the fish of the sea,
whatever passes along the paths of the seas.
(Psalm 8:3–8)

Paul wrote to the church of Corinth, "For a man ought not to cover his head, since he is the image and glory of God" (1 Corinthians 11:7), while James seems to agree: "With it (our tongue) we bless our Lord and Father, and with it we curse people who are made in the likeness of God" (James 3:9).

Again, this isn't speaking specifically to the image as in form, but characteristics that other animals do not have in whole. For instance, there are all kinds of videos out there with examples of how some animals show moral, ethical, and even intellectual abilities, but not to the extent that we find in humans. The abilities to create are there in some form or fashion but not to the extreme that we humans have. An elephant can hold a paintbrush and place paint on canvas but is incapable of creating a masterpiece or taking raw materials and creating a building or something complex like a computer, a phone, or a watch. These are all things only found with those created in the image of God.

But the image goes even deeper than that. Paul wrote in his letter to the Romans, "For what can be known about God is plain to them, because God has shown it to them. For his invisible attributes, namely, his eternal power and divine nature, have been clearly perceived, ever since the creation of the world, in the things that have been made. So they are without excuse" (Romans 1:19–20). Understand what Paul just said right here. We are created in God's image. We are His image bearers. We can see Him within ourselves; we can see clearly what He is like; His invisible attributes. His creative, rational, self-sacrificial attributes are permanently unchanged. Is our image marred by sin? For sure, and we will examine that further in chapter four.

This leads us to the second part of being image bearers. We were created to have dominion over all the earth. God designed everything deliberately, including man in His own image. Jack Cottrell, in his book *The Faith Once For All*, says this:

> Subduing the earth requires the full use of all our creative and rational powers in order to produce and invent such things as wheels, steel, glass, microscopes, telescopes, violins, organs, nuclear reactors, computers, poems, and books. Man's lordship over the earth is not absolute, however. We may be the crown of creation,

but we are still creatures. God alone is the Creator and absolute Lord over all. In our function of dominion we are still God's servants, His stewards. We exercise dominion over the earth not only for our good, but also and primarily for God's glory. (p. 155)

We read above how ancient rulers would create images of themselves to show where they ruled. We need to take a look at the life of Joseph[1] for just a moment to get a valuable look at a fantastic example. Joseph, after being brought out of prison and into Pharaoh's court, interpreted through the Holy Spirit two dreams from Pharaoh. In response, "Pharaoh said to Joseph, 'Since God has shown you all this, there is none so discerning and wise as you are. You shall be over my house, and all my people shall order themselves as you command. Only as regards the throne will I be greater than you.' And Pharaoh said to Joseph, 'See, I have set you over all the land of Egypt'" (Genesis 41:39–41). Then Pharaoh gave Joseph everything he needed in order to be successful.

Pharaoh essentially took Joseph and created him in his own image. When people looked at Joseph, they were to act as if Pharaoh himself had given the order. This is what it means to be in the image of God.

But being image bearers goes beyond this. In the next chapter we will look further into the role of image bearers, namely, how are we to use our image to best glorify God? And we ask an even better question—what is free will?

---

1. See Genesis chapters 37–50.

CHAPTER 3
WHY THE TREE?

Why is it that as Bible-believing, Christ-professing, God-fearing people we think that we can choose to love others, but we cannot *choose* to love God or to follow Jesus? There are more podcasts than you'd have time to listen to and enough books to fill a library on the deeper theological arguments surrounding the topic of free will or libertarian free will.

I have spent a great deal of time studying these and will not be diving down that rabbit hole in this chapter. We are going to follow Paul's command to Timothy, "Have nothing to do with foolish, ignorant controversies; you know that they breed quarrels" (2 Timothy 2:23), and elsewhere, "nor to devote themselves to myths and endless genealogies, which promote speculations rather than the stewardship from God that is by faith" (1 Timothy 1:4). I appreciate how the Amplified Bible writes this, "nor to pay attention to legends (fables, myths) and endless genealogies, which give rise to useless speculation *and* meaningless arguments rather than advancing God's program *of instruction.*" I would call some of the arguments meaningless that don't advance God's kingdom.

Rather, we are going to reason our way through the Scriptures, as is written in the book of Isaiah:

> *Come now, let us reason together*, says the Lord:
> though your sins are like scarlet,
> they shall be as white as snow;
> though they are red like crimson,
> they shall become like wool.
> *If you are willing and obedient,*
> you shall eat the good of the land;
> *but if you refuse and rebel,*
> you shall be eaten by the sword;
> for the mouth of the Lord has spoken.
> (Isaiah 1:18–20, emphasis added)

Note the phrases in italics. These all indicate choice. Similarly, we read in Joshua:

> Now therefore fear the Lord and serve him in sincerity and in faithfulness. Put away the gods that your fathers served beyond the River and in Egypt, and serve the Lord. And if it is evil in your eyes to serve the Lord, *choose this day whom you will serve*, whether the gods your fathers served in the region beyond the River, or the gods of the Amorites in whose land you dwell. But as for me and my house, we will serve the Lord. (Joshua 24:14–15, emphasis added)

Again, note the choice. Throughout the Old Testament, we find God calling out to Israel to "come back," to "be holy," to turn from their wicked ways and choose a different path. If there is a choice, there is free will. Without choice, we are just robots following a script, a line of code, so to speak. But we aren't robots. We were created "in his own image" (Genesis 1:27). In the last chapter, we shared how we are in His image, morally, ethically, and intellectually. But we are created another way in His image: free to make choices.

God didn't have to create; it was His own free will choice. "Our God is in the heavens; he does all that he pleases" (Psalm 115:3). Robots make what seem like choices, but those choices are always within the lines of written code. Their choices are surrounded by red tape, so to speak; they only give the illusion of choice. Take the movie *I Robot*, for instance. According to the rules of robotics in that story, if a robot had to choose between hurting a human and self-sacrifice, the robot must sacrifice itself. The bot may have the illusion of choice, but the rules dictated that choice before it was ever made.

This is how some scholars see free will. They see it as an illusion created by God. But if this is true, then the many times that God called out to His people (Israel) to choose Him were a cruel joke on His part. There would be nothing they could do to come to this God who calls so desperately for His people.

So we go back to the beginning. God is by Himself. Well, He isn't technically alone. He is Three in One. He has all He needs. Yet, there is a longing He has. One to create. To create and to be loved. To create, to be loved by His creation, and to show Himself and all He is to that creation.

So God speaks. He forms all the material universe with but the words from His mouth, "By the word of the Lord the heavens were made, and by the breath of his mouth all their host. For he spoke, and it came to be; he commanded, and it stood firm" (Psalm 33:6, 9). Then comes man. The animals and Earth were created by words, yet man He created with His hands: "then the LORD God formed the man of dust from the ground and breathed into his nostrils the breath of life" (Genesis 2:7).

I want you to take a moment and picture this in your head. It's a thought exercise. I know He didn't literally do this, but picture it anyway. God is standing on the earth. He has surveyed all that He has done so far. It's all good. But it isn't yet complete. So He squats down, takes a little dirt, a bit of water, maybe a bit of clay from the earth, and mixes it all together. Then, like a master potter, He sets out and for hours He uses His fingers and palms to knead, shape, and pull away excess mud. Eventually, this lump of dirt takes form. This is the form of man. God then leans forward and blows the breath of life into this lifeless form. He blows it up like we would blow up a balloon. God smiles, standing up, He looks down and thinks to Himself, "It is complete. My masterpiece is finished." Then God surveyed one more time all the works of His hands and "behold, it was very good" (Genesis 1:31).

Before we move on, we must define a few words. Belief is to have a personal, relational trust in God, based on His revelation through His words and His deeds. A firm trust that brings a reverent fear of the Lord, which then leads to obedience because we know His promises are true and His commands are reliable (Psalm 119:89–91), protective (Psalm 33:18–19), and beneficial (Psalm 31:19).

When we say that God created us in His image to worship, we mean to attribute honor, reverence, or worth to this triune

God. It is fully understood in a relationship where God reveals Himself, His purpose, and His will. Then, through a personal relationship with Him, the one who worships responds with adoration, humility, submission, and obedience to God. Through love (adoration), understanding He is God (belief or faith), and that I am His servant (humility), I can choose to follow Him in obedience and submission.

"Whoever believes in the Son has eternal life; whoever does not obey the Son shall not see life, but the wrath of God remains on him" (John 3:36). This is important to show that belief and obedience are synonymous in Scripture. It is important to understand all of these things so we don't water down the message of Jesus Christ. Belief is not just simply acknowledgment, and worship isn't just singing a song.

We worship God for who He is. We follow all His commandments, acting in obedience, and trusting Him at His word about all He says of Himself. This brings us into full fellowship with God. So why the tree?

"And the LORD God commanded the man, saying, 'You may surely eat of every tree of the garden, but of the tree of the knowledge of good and evil you shall not eat, for in the day that you eat of it you shall surely die'" (Genesis 2:16–17). It's in the middle of Genesis chapter three that we get a picture we often overlook. "And they heard the sound of the LORD God walking in the garden in the cool of the day" (Genesis 3:8). Let's picture this together. It's the Middle East. You are in a beautiful garden, but it's a garden in the middle of one of the hottest parts of the world, so the days are still hot. But as the day wanes, the temperature drops a little. It starts to cool off. Suddenly, there is a breeze. This breeze brings a crisp chill to the air, and there in the distance, you see Him. Oh, your heart lights up. The anticipation is killing you. You know it's that time, and so does He. Between the trees, you see Him. The beginning and end, Alpha and Omega, creator of all things, and He has come to see you!! To "walk in the cool of the day."

Scripture never says how long Adam and Eve were in the garden. I suspect it was at least a few decades. Remember, Adam was a full-grown adult male straight out of the gate. His "walk with God," as many Christians call it today, started day one, and as Genesis records, he lived to be 930 years of age.

Over the years, I have often heard the phrase "my walk with the Lord," or something to that nature, especially from older Christians. What we have failed to see or maybe neglected altogether is that it was always God's plan to walk side by side with His creation. God always wanted a relationship that would go both ways. For a people to commune with Him. He had it perfect for a time. But then the good choices became bad choices. Trust and obedience became a lack of trust and disobedience. Sin would enter the world and separate His creation from Him.

So, why the tree? We still haven't answered that question. A lot of people ask variations of this same question: "If God knew that man would sin, causing death and separation from Him, why place the tree in the garden in the first place?"

The answer, while simple, is so easy to overlook. It was all for love. Love is an action word. It's a decision that moves the lover to action. We as humans often equate love as a feeling or something we can fall into or out of. But that is a lie straight from the devil himself. Love can share feelings or may come with feelings, but love itself is not a feeling. It is a decision. It is an action. Jesus told us to love our enemies and pray for those who persecute us. Did He say you'd have warm, fuzzy feelings or that it wouldn't be difficult?

We need to realize that love, like all decisions, is a choice, conscious or unconscious, like what to wear, what to eat, who to spend time with, or whether to obey. That's right, I said it: obedience is a choice.

So, without the ability to choose between two objects, in this case between God and His will for Adam versus Adam's wants and wishes, there was no chance of true love existing. Adam needed to make the clear choice of his free will, of his rational mind, to follow God and all His commands.

Hence the tree. This gave Adam a clear choice to show, through an action, the true love he had for his creator. God could have written love directly into our DNA (or code) as some would have you believe, but we would be unable to truly love God. Love would become a forced action rather than a free will decision.

CHAPTER 4
THE GREAT FALL

So here we are, made in God's image. Created and formed to show creation that He exists and who He is. We were formed and made to be His ambassadors to the world. To rule over all creation. We were to "subdue the earth" (Genesis 1:28), bringing order to any amount of chaos. To rule with God, to worship God, to walk beside God in true communion. This was His goal, His heart, and our truest, deep-down desire.

We know from Scripture that Adam made the choice to love God with all his heart, soul, and strength. We can know this because sin didn't enter into the equation for quite some time. Adam made a choice and explained to his wife, "Don't eat from this tree." He chose to believe God when He said, "In the day you eat of it you will surely die" (Genesis 2:17).

For years, God had exactly what He wanted. His masterpiece was complete. A creation that chose to love Him of his own accord, forsaking the one and only thing he couldn't have, that tree.

That's right, I said it. Adam had everything: a wife, fulfilling work in the garden, and a real relationship with the one and only creator God. But something terrible happened, something absolutely horrible. Something that we find happens to us to this day. Adam lost faith in his creator.

> Now the serpent was more crafty than any other beast of the field that the LORD God had made. He said to the woman, "Did God actually say, 'You shall not eat of any tree in the garden'?" And the woman said to the serpent, "We may eat of the fruit of the trees in the garden, but God said, 'You shall not eat of the fruit of the tree that is in the midst of the garden, neither shall you touch it, lest you die.'" But the serpent said to the woman, "You will not surely die. For God knows that when you eat of it your eyes will be opened, and you will be like God, knowing good and evil." So when the woman saw that the tree was good for food, and that it was a delight to the eyes, and that the tree was to be desired to make one wise, she took of its fruit and ate, and she also gave some to her husband who was with her, and he ate. Then the eyes of both were opened, and they knew that they were naked. And they sewed fig leaves together and made themselves loincloths. (Genesis 3:1–7)

Paul points back to this story a couple of times in the New Testament. He specifically says Adam sinned (Romans 5:12–14) and Eve was deceived (1 Timothy 2:14). The serpent tricked Eve, but Adam was the one who was personally given the commandment, "Don't eat from this tree" (Genesis 2:17).

We see in the next few verses of Genesis chapter three that a set of curses was placed upon these three transgressors. The serpent was to forevermore crawl on its belly. Eve was to have increased pain during childbirth, and her desire would be for her husband. And Adam was to work the ground by the sweat of his brow to eat and feed his family (Genesis 3:14–19).

But this all goes so much deeper than we tend to read in the narrative of these first few chapters of Genesis. The dominion over the earth that humans had is now gone. The relationship humans had with God is now gone. Death, up until now, was not a concept that Adam and Eve could comprehend, and death had now entered the realm of the living. So let's look at these other things we lost, starting with dominion.

When Adam sinned against God by choosing to disobey His rule, to disbelieve God at His holy Word, to believe God would keep something good from him, Adam gave up all his rights. He forfeited all his power to subdue and his sonship. But who then picked it up?

One might be tempted to give the Sunday School answer, "Jesus." But that would be the wrong answer. Scripture tells us exactly who picked up the power and dominion over the earth and all creation—Satan grasped hold of that power. "The deceiver of the whole world" (Revelation 12:9) holds power over "the whole world" (1 John 5:19). He is "the prince of the power of the air" (Ephesians 2:2), "the god of this world" (2 Corinthians 4:4), and "the ruler of this world" (John 12:31; 14:30).

Adam inadvertently handed over the keys to the whole

Earth to Satan. That is why Satan, during the tempting of Christ in Matthew chapter four, was able to say, "Worship me and I will give it all to you" (Matthew 4:9).

Next, death, which had never been seen until now, entered the scene. Only, this death wasn't just for mankind. Creation itself as a whole began to decay and die (Genesis 3:19; Romans 5:12; 6:23), "For the creation was subjected to futility, not willingly, but because of him who subjected it, in hope that the creation itself will be set free from its bondage to corruption and obtain the freedom of the glory of the children of God" (Romans 8:20–21).

The word *mooth* in Hebrew means "to put to death as a penalty." The Septuagint (Greek Old Testament) uses the word *thanatos*, which can mean both a figurative and literal death. *Thanatos* carries more meaning than just physical death. It includes a sense of mortal danger or dangerous circumstances. Looking at both the Hebrew and Greek words gives us a greater picture of what God was showing within this story. When the serpent told Eve that she "surely would not die," he was essentially telling her there was no immediate danger to her choices. That there wouldn't really be a penalty.

Now, while this event carried with it the ramifications of physical death, that isn't all that was entailed within death itself. This death was about separation. Separation from life in and of itself. Jesus said, "I am the way, and the truth, and the life" (John 14:6). Again, not just a separation from physical life, which most find uncomfortable, but a separation from The Life. As has been said, sin separates us from this good and holy God. He cannot stand to be in the presence of evil, of wickedness, and of unrighteousness.

But still, there is more. Death is both physical and spiritual, but there is a third point to death. Jesus called it "the second death" (Revelation 2:11; 21:8) and said, "do not fear those who kill the body but cannot kill the soul. Rather fear him who can destroy both soul and body in hell" (Matthew 10:28). Physical, spiritual, and eternal death. That is heavy. That one little lie, a twisting of words, "You will surely not die" (Genesis 3:4), only meant immediately. But it's the next verse that Satan still uses today: "For God knows that when you eat of it your eyes will be opened ..." He essentially said, "You can't trust God. You can't believe his words. He just wants to hold you back." Oh, how many people have fallen for that lie.

Lastly, our relationship with God was severed. It became so strained that we hardly read within the pages of Scripture of God walking with another person. The holiness of God restrains Him from being in the presence of sin (Isaiah 59:2). Only on occasion do we see God walking with anyone. We see that Enoch "walked with God" (Genesis 5:24) and that God spoke with Moses "face to face" (Numbers 12:8).

I can only imagine the heartache God must have felt at the moment of the Fall. We know He knew beforehand that this was going to happen. We know that it didn't shock Him. We even know that He knew the second it happened. And yet we read that God walked into the garden and gave Adam and Eve a chance to confess to what they had done (Genesis 3:8–11).

God had everything He wanted until sin entered the equation. Then He lost it all. Yet even in the heartbreak, there was a plan already in place. A plan to redeem that which was lost. To redeem the entire situation. This plan was going to take time to come to completion. But thanks be to God; time is on His side.

CHAPTER 5
REDEMPTION EARLY ON

Don't jump ahead here. There is a plan for redemption, and as a Christian reading this book, you already know the end result, that God sent Jesus. But we have to build up to that result. The plan for redemption started way before Jesus came. The plan began to unfold by following the lineage of Adam.

You may be thinking, "Well, of course it followed Adam. He is the first man after all." That is correct. But the lineage breaks off into branches, much like following a tree from trunk to leaf. It flows from one, it breaks into many, but we follow the story to one set of leaves. We see the Old Testament track the lineage from Adam through specific children until Noah.

Noah was redeemed by God from the destruction of the world by way of a boat. That in and of itself is impressive. We can spend an afternoon excitedly discussing all the different pieces to that puzzle, like how Noah likely didn't have any idea what an ark was, let alone a flood (or did he?). But in an act of willful obedience, a faith that took God at His word, Noah "in reverent fear constructed an ark for the saving of his household" (Hebrews 11:7).

We move on from Noah, through his sons, to Abram. God made a covenant with Abram and changed his name to Abraham. This was a more one-sided covenant than we give credit for. Essentially, God said, "If you'll follow me and me only, I will make you into a great nation and all the world will be blessed through you. Not by your power but my own." God then walked the covenantal sacrifice all by Himself (Genesis 15:1–21). Abraham was supposed to be the one to walk the sacrifice, but by God doing it made a greater statement of "nothing you can do will change this. I'm doing it regardless."

From Abraham we go through Issac to Jacob, who became the nation of Israel through his twelve sons. It would be through this nation that the fulfillment of the plan would take place. Again, as stated at the end of the last chapter, this plan was going to take time. But time is something God doesn't lack because He doesn't dwell within time.

Israel, of course, ends up in Egypt under slavery. The plan starts to unfold more deeply during this period. More specifically, at the end of that period, during the enslavement of Israel. Out of the water came a child who was raised in the home of Egypt's ruler, Pharaoh. This child would eventually lead Israel out of slavery to freedom. This child, of course, is Moses. We walk from Adam to Moses before we begin to see the redemption plan unfold.

What do we mean when we say "redemption" or "redeem"? There are two Greek words used for "redeem." The first is *lytroo*, which describes a person who paid a very high price for the slave of his choice. When Paul used the term in

Titus 2:14, he was explaining the high price Jesus paid for our sins. Essentially, Jesus paid the highest price ever to free a slave. The second word is *exagorazo*, which is a compound word meaning "out of the slave market." It is the image of someone going to the slave market with the sole purpose of purchasing a slave just to release that slave as a free man. So we could say "redemption" means, "an extremely high price paid to free another from slavery."

So what was the extremely high price paid for Israel's freedom? For that, we must look to the book of Exodus. It was a big one. A plague given by God to soften Pharaoh's hardened heart. It was so big that it finally broke him.

> At midnight the LORD struck down all the firstborn in the land of Egypt, from the firstborn of Pharaoh who sat on his throne to the firstborn of the captive who was in the dungeon, and all the firstborn of the livestock. And Pharaoh rose up in the night, he and all his servants and all the Egyptians. And there was a great cry in Egypt, for there was not a house where someone was not dead. Then he summoned Moses and Aaron by night and said, "Up, go out from among my people, both you and the people of Israel; and go, serve the LORD, as you have said. Take your flocks and your herds, as you have said, and be gone, and bless me also!" (Exodus 12:29–32)

The price paid for Israel to be set free was the firstborn of every person and creature in Egypt. We know from the story that Israel was not touched during this plague because they acted in obedience to God when He ordered them to partake in that first Passover meal and place the blood on the door frame. Even after this great disaster, Pharaoh became hesitant. His entire population of forced laborers had just vacated Egypt. So he attempted to chase them down. Here we find a second price paid by Pharaoh to free Israel from enslavement.

> Then the LORD said to Moses, "Stretch out your hand over the sea, that the water may come back upon the Egyptians, upon their chariots, and upon their horsemen." So Moses stretched out his hand over the sea, and the sea returned to its normal course when the morning appeared. And as the Egyptians fled into it, the LORD threw the Egyptians into the midst of the sea. The waters returned and covered the chariots and the horsemen; of all the host of Pharaoh that had followed them into the sea, not one of them remained. (Exodus 14:26–28)

God then took the newly freed people of Israel and proclaimed to them, "Obey my voice, and I will be your God, and you shall be my people. And walk in all the way that I command you, that it may be well with you" (Jeremiah 7:23). God then proceeded to give to Moses the law, which Israel was expected to obey. This became what is known as the Torah, or the first five books of the Bible: the Law of Moses. There are 613 commandments given within these five books. Of those, 248 are "Do this," while 365 are "Do not do this." Most of us are familiar with the Big 10:

1. Have no gods before me.
2. Have no idols.

3. Don't misuse my name.
4. Remember the Sabbath day; keep it holy.
5. Honor your father and mother.
6. Don't murder.
7. Don't commit adultery.
8. Don't steal.
9. Don't bear false witness.
10. Don't covet.

But why the laws? There was no way possible that anyone could maintain this level of perfection. But that is exactly the point. The law was given for a twofold purpose. First, as a teacher, to show just how far man had fallen from God. Second, to bring atonement for the sins of the people.

The law was more of a tutor/teacher, according to the Apostle Paul, "Now before faith came, we were held captive under the law, imprisoned until the coming faith would be revealed. So then, the law was our guardian until Christ came, in order that we might be justified by faith" (Galatians 3:23–24). But he makes it even more profound in Romans chapter seven:

> What then shall we say? That the law is sin? By no means! Yet if it had not been for the law, I would not have known sin. For I would not have known what it is to covet if the law had not said, "You shall not covet." But sin, seizing an opportunity through the commandment, produced in me all kinds of covetousness. For apart from the law, sin lies dead. I was once alive apart from the law, but when the commandment came, sin came alive and I died. The very commandment that promised life proved

> to be death to me. For sin, seizing an opportunity through the commandment, deceived me and through it killed me. So the law is holy, and the commandment is holy and righteous and good. (Romans 7:7–12)

Paul says here that God needed to show humanity just how depraved we had become. How sin and death had changed us. You probably know people who don't believe in God and disbelieve that they are bad in any way. Many will say things like, "I'm a generally good person." And yet, when we examine the Scriptures, we find that "no one is good, no not one" (Psalms 14:1–3; 53:1–3; Romans 3:10–12). Paul continues:

> Did that which is good, then, bring death to me? By no means! It was sin, producing death in me through what is good, in order that sin might be shown to be sin, and through the commandment might become sinful beyond measure. For we know that the law is spiritual, but I am of the flesh, sold under sin. For I do not understand my own actions. For I do not do what I want, but I do the very thing I hate. (Romans 7:13–15)

So Paul reiterates that the law was given to show us what sin is. How can I know right from wrong without someone teaching me? It's funny to say that, because that was one of the lies the serpent told Eve, "You'll know good and evil" (Genesis 3:5). Take children, for instance. No one has to teach them how to hit, bite, or lie, but we must teach them discipline, sharing, and kindness. Now we understand why we act as we do.

Because the sin within us fights against the good we want to do. Our flesh and our spirit are in conflict. As the old saying goes, "There are two wolves within you. The one you feed is the one that wins."

> Now if I do what I do not want, I agree with the law, that it is good. So now it is no longer I who do it, but sin that dwells within me. For I know that nothing good dwells in me, that is, in my flesh. For I have the desire to do what is right, but not the ability to carry it out. For I do not do the good I want, but the evil I do not want is what I keep on doing. Now if I do what I do not want, it is no longer I who do it, but sin that dwells within me. (Romans 7:16–20)

We will get more into this topic later, but we find it necessary to state here that, though sin dwells within us and temptation comes our way at an almost mind-boggling rate, we have a great high priest who knows what it is like to be tempted in every way imaginable (Hebrews 4:15), who speaks on our behalf (Romans 8:34), who is quick to forgive and will help us if we ask (1 John 1:9).

> So I find it to be a law that when I want to do right, evil lies close at hand. For I delight in the law of God, in my inner being, but I see in my members another law waging war against the law of my mind and making me captive to the law of sin that dwells in my members. Wretched man that I am! Who will deliver me from this body of death? (Romans 7:21–24)

Paul was a firm believer that we could learn from and understand every command of God: "All Scripture is breathed out by God and profitable for teaching, for reproof, for correction, and for training in righteousness, that the man of God may be complete, equipped for every good work" (2 Timothy 3:16–17). Not that we fall under the law, but it shows us, again, how far we have fallen and how far we have to go to reach perfection. We will discuss more later about being "holy, for I am holy" (1 Peter 1:16) and working "out your own salvation with fear and trembling" (Philippians 2:12).

The second thing the law did was bring a level of atonement. An atonement is reparation for an offense or injury. It's the act that brings reconciliation between God and man.

God as creator is the one who sets the terms and conditions for the contract, much like a judge in a courtroom. In the next chapter, we will dive deeper into the meaning and purpose of atonement.

CHAPTER 6
ATONEMENT

As stated at the end of the last chapter, atonement is the reparation for an offense or injury. It comes from the combination of two words: "at" and "onement." If you're like me, you're asking right now, "What is 'onement'? That sounds like a made-up word." So we pull out our big red buddy, the dictionary, which tells us that "onement" is the state of "being at one" or reconciled. So, putting these words together, we could say that atonement is repayment for offense or injury, bringing reconciliation between two parties. In this case, we are speaking of God and humanity.

God is the one who sets the terms of repayment. He, as the creator of all this, has that full right. So, atonement is His plan to bring the human race back into alignment with His will. This, like everything else we've learned up until now, depends upon the free will actions of His creation: the decision to do exactly as He said, fulfilling the prescription given.

Atonement can be summed up like this: Sin violates the

holiness of God, which brings the sentence of death and separation from this holy God. Because of God's wrath regarding sin, these two penalties are established. The only way to appease the wrath of God is by the substitution of another's death. If the penalty for sin is death, something or someone must die to pay that cost. So God gave the sacrificial offerings as a way for sinful people to receive blessings from God rather than judgment. In His loving kindness, He gave a way out for all who sin against Him.

We see animal sacrifices being used within Scripture long before Moses was given the sacrificial law. We see this with Abel (Genesis 4:2–4; Hebrews 11:4), Noah (Genesis 8:20), the Patriarchs Abraham, Isaac, and Jacob (Genesis 13:18; 26:25; 33:20; 35:7), and Job, who gave sacrifices for the sins of his children (Job 1:5).

Sacrificial atonement becomes more prevalent as we walk through the book of Exodus and into the next three books of the law (Leviticus, Numbers, and Deuteronomy). At the first Passover, blood was spread onto the doorposts of every home belonging to the nation of Israel. This acted as a protective barrier, so to speak, protecting the nation from the coming judgment of death. When the angel of the Lord saw the blood, he passed over that home, and no harm would befall those inside.

What we see when we study the books of Moses is that God set up a great many sacrifices. This is because God's wrath against sin is so strong. While we as Christians constantly praise God for His great mercy and loving kindness, we must never forget that God is also wrathful against all unholiness. The writer of Hebrews states that priests were to pour out the blood of the sacrifices on the tent and every vessel for worship, and that each needed to be purified with blood. "Indeed, under the law almost everything is purified with blood, and without the shedding of blood there is no forgiveness of sin" (Hebrews 9:19–22).

Leviticus chapters one through seven give a variety of sacrifices, including whole burnt offerings, guilt offerings, and sin offerings. These show us that, to God, sin is a chief concern and one that must be handled. Sin cannot stand before this good and holy God. So, without appropriate sacrifices, man cannot stand before Him.

The greatest example of the Old Testament sacrifice is the Day of Atonement. On this day, God sets an intricate set of rituals to pay for the sins of the entire nation. There are three main steps involved:

1. The Chief Priest must make atonement for himself first and foremost (Leviticus 16:11–14). Without it, the priest might die in the presence of the Holy of Holies and thus fail in bringing atonement for the nation.
2. The Chief Priest must offer the first of two goats. This one is a sin offering for the people. Its blood is sprinkled on the mercy seat, symbolizing the divine side of atonement (Leviticus 16:15–19). God's holy justice is satisfied by the sprinkling of this blood before Him.
3. The Chief Priest now lays his hands on the second goat, the scapegoat. As he prays for the sins of the people, their sins are transferred upon the goat by the Chief Priest. It is then set free to wander the

> wilderness to "carry on itself all their sins" (Leviticus 16:20–22).

By this, the people would be cleansed of the defilement that sin has left upon them. The two goats show there are two sides to the atonement. The first side is how to free people of sin and its defilement. The second shows the appeasement of God's holy wrath. Within Christianity, we often overlook the first while wholly focusing on the latter. We focus primarily on the propitiation or appeasement of divine wrath. But the sacrificial system was designed to both satisfy judgment and to remove the guilt of sin from the sinner.

One thing that has always shocked me is the sheer number of animal sacrifices necessary to appease the wrath of God. There were daily, weekly, monthly, yearly, and extra special sacrifices. Sacrifices for known and unknown sins, personal and national sins. The sheer number of bulls, male and female goats, male and female sheep, and birds necessary to make this happen was astronomical.

Of course, we do learn two things from this. The first being just how greatly God hates sin. The second is that Israel never truly followed through with this instruction. But even when they did follow the prescription to the letter, we find the prophets of God often telling the entire nation to stop performing the sacrifices. This was because the people were forgetting a major detail needed for atonement to take place correctly.

"I have had enough of burnt offerings ... I do not delight in the blood of bulls ... Bring no more vain offerings" (Isaiah 1:11, 13). God used similar wording through Jeremiah, Amos, and Malachi. In Malachi, He stated it this way, "Oh that there were one among you who would shut the doors, that you might not kindle fire on my altar in vain! I have no pleasure in you, says the Lord of hosts, and I will not accept an offering from your hands" (Malachi 1:10).

What caused the creator to speak in such a manner? The people followed the rituals but not the heart of sacrifice. Sacrificial rituals only atone for those who genuinely turn from sin and humble themselves before God. Nothing less than inward sincerity will bring reconciliation between God and sinful man.

The sacrificial system was never intended to be perfect or permanent. Just like the law, it was intended to show the imperfections found in fallen humanity and what must be done to reconcile the strained relationship between the perfect creator and an imperfect creation, namely, fallen man.

To that point, the sacrificial system was a huge success, but it would take a perfect sacrifice to bring perfect atonement. One that the prophet Isaiah spoke of in much of Isaiah chapters fifty-two and fifty-three. This servant from the house of David would be wounded for our transgressions, bruised for our iniquities, the Lord would lay on Him all the iniquities of His people, making this sacrifice the perfect guilt offering for all the people of God (Isaiah 53:5, 6, 10).

CHAPTER 7
IN STEPS JESUS

From the time Moses put chisel to stone until the birth of Jesus was somewhere between 1,400 and 1,600 years. That means for 1,000–1,200 years God begged Israel to listen to His voice. We read through the prophets Him repeating the words, "If you will listen to my voice" (Isaiah 28:23). He begged them to turn from their wicked ways, to embrace a true, right relationship with the creator of all. After the exile, the nation had successfully killed off every prophet God sent to them, so He went silent. Or at least silent on paper. We have nearly 400 years where there is no writing whatsoever of the words of God.

After nearly 4,000 years since Adam first allowed the curse of sin and death to enter the mortal world, the time had come to finish that original plan for redemption. The plan to bring God and man back together. The law had done what it set out to do, for no word from God returns to Him empty (Isaiah 55:11). It showed the world how far it had fallen and its need for redemption. But the law could never fulfill perfect redemption. For that to take place would be an act that only God could take care of.

"The Word became flesh and dwelt among us" (John 1:14). In chapter one we discussed how this Word was, is, and always will be God. The Word is Jesus. He is that perfect one sent to realign imperfect humanity with perfect creator.

One of the most difficult things to wrap our minds around today is the concept of the virgin birth. In Luke chapter one we read of the Angel Gabriel speaking to a young, betrothed woman named Mary. He proclaims that she will have a son, not born of man but by the Spirit. But rather than huff and puff like so many today might, a "That's not possible" kind of thing, Mary responds with "Let it be to me according to your word" (Luke 1:38).

Many would balk like Zechariah did upon the announcement that Elizabeth would bear him a child, but Mary responded with humility and trust. Today, many atheists and Christians alike have begun to balk at the idea of the virgin birth. Caricatures like "The greatest lie ever told" are now being passed around like some type of joke. Why do we struggle so much as humans with the idea of specific miracles?

If this same God did all the wondrous miracles, signs, and wonders written about in the Bible, such as healing the blind, the deaf, the mute, and raising the dead, why do we struggle to think He cannot possibly do this?

Perhaps it is because it bypasses all biological science. But so do many other miracles witnessed even today. Old people having children. Brain tumors just vanishing after years of scans. Barren women giving birth. These types of things don't just happen on their own. So this same God, who can do all these other things, says He can and will cause a virgin to be with child without the aid of a man, that the child would be born both God and man, I'm not arguing with Him. He said it. He did it. I trust Him.

But why? Why break the laws of biology? Was it just to show He could? No, it goes so much deeper than that. To atone for sin, blood must be spilled. Death must take place. It's been stated throughout this book that God had a plan. A plan for perfect redemption, to pay the purchasing price in full. This price must be eternal, permanent, everlasting. Jesus was able to pay such a penalty once for all time because He was, and is, God. There is no more perfect sacrifice than the blood of the creator Himself. Paying the penalty for sin through His death. Freeing sinners from the bondage of sin. Appeasing the divine wrath of this good and holy God.

So the purpose of the virgin birth was that God, who has no form, could take the form of man, allowing formless deity to have lifeblood which could be spilled at the proper time. What's even more impressive is that Jesus knew all of this from a young age (Luke 2:49; 22:42–44).

We can see it was necessary for Jesus to be God. But this begs the question, "Why a baby?" God could have come to Earth as a visible manifestation of deity. He had done so with Abraham (Genesis 18). But this just wouldn't be the same. He could have just appeared as a thirty-year-old man and been killed all the same for "blasphemy against God," but it just wouldn't have been the same.

"And the Word became flesh and dwelt among us" (John 1:14). Why the baby? Why a human? To prove that it could be done as a human. He did this for two very important reasons.

First, He had to come as a baby to grow up feeling the

same things we feel as humans. "For we do not have a high priest who is unable to sympathize with our weaknesses, but one who in every respect has been tempted as we are, yet without sin" (Hebrews 4:15). God the Father can never be tempted in the same way we are. Never has been, never will be. Not, at least, when it comes to the temptation of sin. But Jesus, who intercedes on our behalf to the Father (Romans 8:34), can tell Him, "Send wisdom and grace to that one, I know what it is like to be betrayed by a friend," or "Send comfort, I know what it's like to lose a loved one," or "Give that one your strength, I know what it's like to be tempted by Satan."

The second person of the Trinity was tempted by Satan just like we are daily, and yet walked away without falling prey to his schemes! As Jesus ended His forty-day fast in the wilderness, being tempted by the enemy, the angels surrounded Him to bring comfort and to minister to Him. I imagine Him saying, "I did it. I beat him. Not as God, but I beat him as a man." Remember, while Jesus was fully God, He was also fully man, and He "did not count equality with God a thing to be grasped, but emptied himself, by taking the form of a servant, being born in the likeness of men" (Philippians 2:6–7).

This tells us it was a decision. A life choice, if you will. He chose to give up His glorious stature. The word we translate as "empty" in Philippians 2:7 is the word *kenoo*, and it has only one meaning in Greek: to make empty or void. *Kenoo* makes this a picture of a king who wanted to know what the people thought of him. So he removed his kingly attire, put on the clothing of a pauper, and then hid among the masses to learn all he could from the people. He never stopped being the king but lived under the rules of a pauper. If he used any of his kingliness, then he would never experience life as one of his people. "Therefore he had to be made like his brothers in every respect, so that he might become a merciful and faithful high priest in the service of God, to make propitiation for the sins of the people. For because he himself has suffered when tempted, he is able to help those who are being tempted" (Hebrews 2:17–18).

So to recap, if Jesus wasn't born a baby, He could never grow, learning all the temptations that man deals with. All the different lies that Satan whispers and tries to trick us with. He suffered through life the way we must.

The second part of the "why human" question is this. Man was the one who destroyed the relationship and gave dominion and power over to Satan, so by man, Satan must be defeated:

Therefore, just as sin came into the world through one man, and death through sin, and so death spread to all men because all sinned … for if many died through one man's trespass, much more have the grace of God and the free gift by the grace of that one man Jesus Christ abounded for many. And the free gift is not like the result of that one man's sin. For the judgment following one trespass brought condemnation, but the free gift following many trespasses brought justification. For if, because of one man's trespass, death reigned through that one man, much more will those who receive the abundance of grace and the free gift of righteousness reign in life through the one man Jesus Christ. Therefore, as one trespass led to condemnation for all men, so one act of righteousness leads to justification and life for all men. For as by the one man's disobedience the many were made sinners, so by the one man's obedience the many will be made righteous. (Romans 5:12, 15–19)

Jesus had to be fully God and fully man in order to be that perfect sacrifice, defeating once and for all the power of sin and death. As Paul wrote in 1 Corinthians, death came through man, so through man death needed to be defeated. So through Adam all died; through Christ men are made alive (1 Corinthians 15:21–22).

In the last chapter, we talked about the Old Testament sacrificial law for atonement. In the New Testament, we get to see the fulfillment of Isaiah's prophecy of the suffering servant and David's prophecy found in Psalm 22:

(Psalm 22:1–8)
My God, my God, why have you forsaken me?
Why are you so far from saving me, from the words of
    my groaning?

                                  [Matthew 27:46; Mark 15:34]

O my God, I cry by day, but you do not answer,
and by night, but I find no rest.
Yet you are holy, enthroned on the praises of Israel.
In you our fathers trusted;
they trusted, and you delivered them.
To you they cried and were rescued;
in you they trusted and were not put to shame.
But I am a worm and not a man,

scorned by mankind and despised by the people.
All who see me mock me;
they make mouths at me; they wag their heads;

> [Isaiah 53:3; Matthew 27:29–30, 39;
> Mark 15:18–19; Luke 23:36–37]

"He trusts in the Lord; let him deliver him;
let him rescue him, for he delights in him!"

> [Matthew 27:40–43; Mark 15:29–32;
> Luke 23:35]

(Psalm 22:14–15)
I am poured out like water,
and all my bones are out of joint;
my heart is like wax;
it is melted within my breast;

> [John 19:28]

my strength is dried up like a potsherd,
and my tongue sticks to my jaws;
you lay me in the dust of death

> [Isaiah 53:7; John 19:37]

(Psalm 22:17–18)
I can count all my bones—

they stare and gloat over me;

[Luke 23:27, 35]

they divide my garments among them,
and for my clothing they cast lots.

[John 19:23–24]

(Psalm 22:31)
They shall come and proclaim his righteousness to a
 people yet unborn,
that he has done it.

[John 19:30]

Why this day? Why this time? To be perfectly honest, other than speculation, we can't know for certain. Likely, it was because the Romans had perfected death by crucifixion. For this sacrifice to fulfill the whole sacrificial law, all the blood was to be drained. There was no one better at bloodletting than the Romans. As we read the story, we can understand why Pilot was surprised at Jesus being dead only a few hours into the crucifixion, yet they seemed to forget the beating He took at their hands, causing every drop of blood to be poured out.

Yet He never once questioned His role. He may have asked the Father to take the cup from Him, but He never questioned His role and even stated to His disciples that there is no greater love than to lay down one's life for his friends (John 15:13). Jesus set His eyes on the prize and didn't quit till it was finished: "for the joy that was set before him [Jesus] endured the cross, despising the shame, and is seated at the right hand of the throne of God" (Hebrews 12:2). It is finished, the atonement paid in full once and for all.

CHAPTER 8
THE HARDWORKING HOLY SPIRIT

Once Jesus was crucified, died, buried, and resurrected, death was defeated forever. This specifically refers to the spiritual death, and for those who choose to believe in Jesus, the second death. Remember what we said in chapter three: "Belief is to have a personal, relational trust in God, based on His revelation through His words and His deeds. A firm trust that brings a reverent fear of the Lord, which then leads to obedience because we know His promises are true and His commands are reliable, protective, and beneficial" (p. 18). Paul wrote, "because, if you confess with your mouth that Jesus is Lord and believe in your heart that God raised him from the dead, you will be saved. For with the heart one believes and is justified, and with the mouth one confesses and is saved" (Romans 10:9–10).

Because of His work on the cross, God received back that most prized and priceless item He lost for millennia, the ability to have a relationship with His creation once more. But how He chooses to have that relationship looks very different now than we find in Genesis chapter three. Rather than literally walking in the garden with His creation, God now chooses to dwell within His creation.

"In that day you will know that I am in my Father, and you in me, and I in you. Whoever has my commandments and keeps them, he it is who loves me. And he who loves me will be loved by my Father, and I will love him and manifest myself to him" (John 14:20–21). "I do not ask for these only, but also for those who will believe in me through their word, that they may all be one, just as you, Father, are in me, and I in you, that they also may be in us, so that the world may believe that you have sent me" (John 17:20–21).

Jesus' statement has profound importance. The triangle has now become a square. I am not at all equating believers with God. What I am saying is, the Holy Trinity now dwells in us as believers, and we dwell within Him. But how does this occur? How did the three become one with us? Through the working of the Holy Spirit.

Jesus spent much time speaking to the disciples about the Holy Spirit, sharing with them the role the Holy Spirit would take, the works He would do, and even how He would do it. As we will see below, the Holy Spirit was sent to help, to dwell within us, to comfort, to teach, and to speak everything He hears from the Father.

"I will ask the Father, and he will give you another Helper, to be with you forever, even the Spirit of truth, whom the world cannot receive, because it neither sees him nor knows him. You know him, for he dwells with you and will be in you" (John 14:16–17).

"But the Helper, the Holy Spirit, whom the Father will

send in my name, he will teach you all things and bring to your remembrance all that I have said to you" (John 14:26).

"But when the Helper comes, whom I will send to you from the Father, the Spirit of truth, who proceeds from the Father, he will bear witness about me" (John 15:26).

"Nevertheless, I tell you the truth: it is to your advantage that I go away, for if I do not go away, the Helper will not come to you. But if I go, I will send him to you. And when he comes, he will convict the world concerning sin and righteousness and judgment" (John 16:7–8).

"When the Spirit of truth comes, he will guide you into all the truth, for he will not speak on his own authority, but whatever he hears he will speak, and he will declare to you the things that are to come" (John 16:13).

The Spirit does so much more than just dwell within us. The Spirit brings comfort, teaches us, tells us what to say, speaks for us when needed, gives out gifts, and helps us to pray. He emboldens us to speak powerfully just as He empowered the first church to speak boldly during persecution. He fills us with fruits that make us look more like our Savior (Galatians 5:22–24). Yet we so often overlook the Holy Spirit in our prayers. We are so quick to thank the Father, to thank Jesus (as we should), to make our requests known to these two persons of the Trinity, all the while neglecting the person and work of the Holy Spirit who dwells in us.

Hear what Paul says about the person of the Holy Spirit: "In him you also, when you heard the word of truth, the gospel of your salvation, and believed in him, were sealed with the promised Holy Spirit, who is the guarantee of our inheritance until we acquire possession of it, to the praise of his glory" (Ephesians 1:13–14).

While the majority of Paul's language here speaks like an adopted son knowing full well he has an inheritance coming, it is so much deeper than that and we cannot overlook it. In the Amplified Bible, verse fourteen reads like this, "The Spirit is the guarantee [the first installment, the pledge, a foretaste] of our inheritance until the redemption of *God's own* [purchased] possession [His believers], to the praise of His glory" (Ephesians 1:14 AMP).

This word we translated guarantee is the Greek word *arrhabon*, which means earnest. An earnest was used as a down payment, but also "can be used to indicate an engagement ring. As Christ is the bridegroom and the church is the bride, so the Holy Spirit is the down payment, the earnest money in the long-awaited marriage of the two" (Amplified Bible study notes). The Holy Spirit is the engagement ring on the finger of His bride as a promise to one day be joined with her permanently.

This is a most important picture. God lost mankind due to sin, sacrificed Himself for mankind to free us from slavery, then said, "I'm not ever going to lose you again. Here is my promise, my guarantee, that I am coming back to get you." It's the same picture of Hosea redeeming his wife from the slavery of prostitution that she had reentered on her own (Hosea 3).

The Holy Spirit takes His role seriously. Convicting the world of sin, comforting the afflicted and hurting, handing out gifts as the Father sees fit, praying and interceding on our behalf, giving encouragement, pointing us back to the narrow road when we veer off course, and yet still finding the time to give wisdom and words to say in our times of need. According to James, when we seek wisdom, all we need to do is ask of

God (through the Holy Spirit), who will give it freely (James 1:5).

In my opinion, Jesus and the Holy Spirit are two sides to the same holy gift, the best gift ever given to humanity. A way for redemption through Jesus, and a way to relationship through the Holy Spirit. Again, thanks to the work of Christ on Calvary and the Holy Spirit who dwells within us, God has back that thing He always wanted—a relationship with His creation that can now be eternal once more.

CHAPTER 9
WHERE DO WE GO FROM HERE?

This book was written to be a guiding light to the full knowledge of who God is (Colossians 2:2–3); His full wants and wishes for His creation; the roles and workings of Jesus and the Holy Spirit and how they fulfill the will of God the Father. What you have read has not come from the minds of brilliant men, but from a humble follower of Jesus who is in love with God and His holy word. I have made no claims of my own, but only what is found in Scripture (2 Corinthians 4:5).

It was written because the time has come when people will not endure sound teaching, but having itching ears they have accumulated for themselves teachers to suit their own passions, and turned from listening to the truth, wandering off into myths (2 Timothy 4:3–4).

It was written to destroy all arguments and poor opinions about who God is (2 Corinthians 10:5), not from an attempt to deceive anyone, but to be found approved by God, who has entrusted us with His good news. So I have not spoken to be a pleaser of men, but of God who tests hearts. God is witness; I haven't come with flattery, in a spirit of greed, or seeking glory from people. Only with the simple wish to encourage, exhort, and charge each reader to live in a manner worthy of God, who calls us to His kingdom and glory (1 Thessalonians 2:3–6, 11–12).

I seek that all who read this will take what is written to heart. Allow the Holy Spirit to change your thinking about how to walk and please God. For this is His will for all: sanctification. God has not called us to impurity, but to holiness. So do not disregard any of what you have read, for it was not given by men but God, who gave His Holy Spirit to you (1 Thessalonians 4:1–8).

Every idea found in this book is also found in Scripture. It is backed up by the holy word of God. We know that Scripture didn't come from man, but from God, written by men who were carried along by the Holy Spirit (2 Peter 1:20–21). It is all "breathed out by God and profitable for teaching, for reproof, for correction, and for training in righteousness, that the man of God may be complete, equipped for every good work" (2 Timothy 3:16–17).

As we end here, I ask that you hear what the Holy Spirit is saying through His holy word:

Repent. Turn from your ways to salvation. Repentance leads to salvation (2 Corinthians 7:10). You were bought with an extremely high price (1 Corinthians 7:23), so you are no longer a slave, but a child of God, and if a child, you are an heir to God and co-heir with Christ (Galatians 4:7; Romans 8:17). Understand this: There is no temptation that has overtaken you that is not common to man. Yet God is faithful and will not let you be tempted beyond your ability, if you rely on Him, but during temptation He will provide the way of escape, that you may endure it (1 Corinthians 10:13).

So as obedient children, do not be conformed to the passions of your former self, but be holy, for God is holy (1 Peter 1:14–16). Test everything, hold fast to what is good. Abstain from every form of evil (1 Thessalonians 5:21–22; Romans 12:9). Walk by the Spirit, and you will not gratify the desires of the flesh (Galatians 5:16). For if we go on sinning deliberately after receiving the knowledge of the truth, there no longer remains a sacrifice for sins (Hebrews 10:26). And those who belong to Christ Jesus have crucified the flesh with its passions and desires (Galatians 5:24). If you are attentive, you will see that the one who sows to his own flesh will from the flesh reap corruption, but the one who sows to the Spirit will from the Spirit reap eternal life (Galatians 6:8).

So, you must no longer walk as those in the world do, in the futility of their minds, and give no opportunity to the devil (Ephesians 4:17, 27), for he is a roaring lion, on the prowl, seeking whom he may devour (1 Peter 5:8). Do not grieve the Holy Spirit of God, by whom you were sealed for the day of redemption (Ephesians 4:30).

Therefore, be imitators of God, as beloved children, taking no part in the unfruitful works of darkness, but instead exposing them (Ephesians 5:1, 11), that He might sanctify you, having cleansed you by the washing of water with the word, so that He might present His church to Himself in splendor, without spot or wrinkle or any such thing, that she might be holy and without blemish (Ephesians 5:26–27; Philippians 2:14–15).

I have full knowledge that I am not perfect either and will

not be perfect on this side of heaven, but I will keep pressing forward (Philippians 3:12–14). I acknowledge that we who fully trust in Jesus as commanded in Scripture and explained in the pages of this book are saved, are being saved, and will one day be fully saved (Hebrews 9:27–28), and He, who is faithful and just, will sanctify us completely, making our whole spirit and soul and body blameless at the coming of our Lord Jesus. He is truly faithful and will do it (1 Thessalonians 5:23–24).

So if you have been raised with Christ, seek the things above. Set your mind on things above and not on earthly things. For you have died, and your life is hidden in God through Christ (Colossians 3:1–3). So put off that old self with its practices and put on the new self, which is being renewed in knowledge after the image of its creator (Colossians 3:8–10). And put on, rather, the fullness that comes through the fruits of the Spirit (Galatians 5:22–23).

Keep the commandments unstained and free from reproach (1 Timothy 6:13–15). Do your best to present yourself to God as one approved, a worker who has no need to be ashamed, rightly handling the word of truth (2 Timothy 2:15). Therefore, put away all filthiness and rampant wickedness and receive with meekness the implanted word, which is able to save your souls. Be doers of the word, and not hearers only, and "keep oneself unstained from the world" (James 1:21–22, 26–27).

Finally, whatever is true, honorable, just, pure, lovely, and commendable; if there is any excellence or anything worthy of praise, think about these things. What you have learned, read, and received from the pages of this book, dwell on these things, on walking in love, and on everything that is good

(Philippians 4:8–9; 2 John 1:6; 3 John 11) that again your hearts may be encouraged and reach the full understanding of who God is in all His mystery, through Christ, in whom are hidden all the treasures of knowledge and wisdom (Colossians 2:2–3).

Seeing all these changes in your life, moving from sin to holiness, is not an act of works, hoping to be saved, for works cannot save, but works like these prove a faith that is true (James 2:14, 17–18, 24; 2 Peter 1:3–7).

In closing, I urge you to be like the Berean church, who searched the Scriptures diligently, daily, to see if what Paul had told them was true (Acts 17:11). Do the same with everything you've read throughout this book and especially this last chapter. Always be mindful of the teachers you choose to listen to or follow; many have turned out to be false teachers and wolves in sheep's clothing (2 Peter 2:15, 17–21).

In Christ

www.ingramcontent.com/pod-product-compliance
Lightning Source LLC
Chambersburg PA
CBHW030225170426
43194CB00007BA/870